This workbook belongs t

I give myself permission to:

The impact I have on this world is:

Date:

"Take the first step even though you do not see the entire staircase."

— Dr. Martin Luther King, Jr.

Empowering The Mind

Mindset Workbook and Journal

Designed intentionally for you by:

Nicole Smith, M.Ed.

CEO/Founder, Leadership Coach, Consultant

JMS | CREATIVE LEADERSHIP SOLUTIONS

www.jmscreatesleaders.com | © 2021 JMS Creative Leadership Solutions

Copyright © 2021 by JMS Creative Leadership Solutions

All rights reserved. No part of this publication be reproduced, distributed or transmitted in any form by any means, including photocopying, recording, or other electronic or mechanical methods, without the prior written permission of the publisher, except in the case of brief quotations embodied in critical reviews and certain noncommercial use permitted by copyright law.

Limit of Liability/Disclaimer of Warranty: The advice and strategies contained herein may not be suitable for your situation. You should consult with a professional where appropriate. Neither the publisher not the author should be liable for any loss of profit or any other damages, including but not limited to, special, incidental, consequential or other damages.

Paperback ISBN: 978-0-578-84940-9

HAVE QUESTIONS OR NEED GUIDANCE?
CONTACT JMS CREATIVE LEADERSHIP SOLUTIONS

Business Phone: 704-248-6212
nicolesmith@jmscreatesleaders.com
www.jmscreatesleaders.com

"...just for you!"
a NOTE FROM THE AUTHOR
WELCOME, MY BEAUTIFUL FRIEND.

What I have learned my 25 years in the corporate jungle, I am sharing with you, just for you! How did I manage? What are those lessons? Here is lesson #1. I learned that mindset is EVERYTHING!

Your mindset is, without a doubt, is your greatest asset. It is worth more than any training. It is more valuable than any degree, any education, any job references. It is capable of earning more in one year than any doctor, dentist or investor.

Identifying and overcoming your own specific mindset blocks is one of the most effective ways to completely transform your mindset and level up! Being on the journey of becoming the best version of yourself takes a Growth Mindset, Courage, and Heart and I am proud of you! Let's walk this journey together with intention and courage.

Learn more about me here: jmscreatesleaders.com

Nicole Smith
LEADERSHIP & EI-EQ COACH

Nicole Smith
Founder of JMS Creative Leadership Solutions

JMS

Table of Contents

- Section 1 pg 5

    Start Walking the Journey!

- Section 2 pg 19

    Mindset is everything

- Section 3 pg 29

    Affirmations (Speak it!)

- Section 4 pg 47

    Emotions affecting your mindset

- Section 5 pg 57

    Plan your mindset shift

- Additional Writing Material pg 64

"Mindset is everything. Your mindset will determine your success."
— Nicole Smith

START WALKING THE JOURNEY!

SECTION ONE
workbook

This journal is to help you **improve your mindset, to help you create impact**. The simple practice of writing improves mental clarity, offers the ability to see the big picture of our lives, and serves as a catalogue of every success we've ever had. Tracking and writing your thoughts down allows you to transfer the problem **from your head to paper.** This empties the mind, allowing allocation of precious resources to problem-solving rather than problem-storing.

As a positive consequence of improving your mental clarity, you become more open to insights you may have missed before. As you write your thoughts out, you're essentially having a dialogue with yourself. Writing your thoughts down allows you to see how you've changed over time, so you can see where you did things right, and where you took a misstep and fell. It's impossible not to grow when it comes to writing. That's what makes journal writing such a powerful tool, you'll eventually **see yourself growing as a person.** You will see your mindset shifting. Mindset is daily work, however.

Unlock your potential. Create a greater impact!

This journal gives you writing prompts to **transform your thinking and shift your mindset**. Furthermore, you want to make it a habit to talk about the things that are going well in your life instead of complaining and talking about your problems. This will encourage a mindset of abundance instead of fear and lack. This journal will encourage you to write down all of the little achievements you make throughout the day and week to give yourself a sense of movement. At any moment, you'll be able to look back at what you've accomplished, and realize that, most likely, you are at a better place than you were last month, last week, or even yesterday.

Unlock your potential. Create a greater impact!

7 STEPS

LET'S WALK IN YOUR JOURNEY

Steps: Read each point!

- ✓ **Mindset work is everyday.** Use the daily writing prompts to generate positive thoughts, remove negative thoughts, understand your emotions and triggers and where to improve. Speak kind to yourself. The first worksheet begins with some questions to gain clarity, generate thought on your goals and your mindset as of today. You may have to come back and answer at different points of this journey - that's ok.

- ✓ **Mindset work is everyday. Take** a moment to affirm and manifest your positive thoughts and goals. We have provided affirmations or use the ones you created. Say them out loud!

- ✓ **Mindset work is everyday.** Gain clarity on how your emotions play into your mindset. Thoughts create emotions, which drive your behavior. Learn how to label your emotions and use powerful words to increase your emotional vocabulary.

Unlock your potential. Create a greater impact!

7 STEPS

LET'S WALK IN YOUR JOURNEY

Steps: Read each point!

- [x] **Mindset work is everyday.** Use the daily mindset tracker provided to see your mindset shift gaining a growth mindset, abundance mindset, or a grateful mindset to name a few. Print a few copies.

- [x] **Mindset work is everyday.** Use the weekly planner to organize your time and your individual days. It will give you a sense of accomplishment or insight on where to improve. Every day is a new day!

- [x] **Discuss with your coach**... don't have a coach, let me know.

- [x] **Enjoy your day!**

"Sometimes you know what want and what to do, but it still feels hard to start."

Unlock your potential. Create a greater impact!

Growth Mindset

Continuously learn in every situation. Everything that happens to you is a form of instruction. You just have to pay close attention. Individuals who believe their talents can be developed through hard work, good strategies, constructive feedback from others have a growth mindset. There is a consistent feeling of empowerment, motivation, and a commitment to achieving much more than a fixed mindset. Growth mindset focuses on awareness, perspective, and action. You see everything as an opportunity, you embrace failure, and overcome judgement. Growth as an individual defines the growth of anything you are trying to accomplish.

Courage

Courage is showing up, standing up, and speaking your truth and yes, it will be uncomfortable. Yet, having courage also means showing up when you can't *control the outcome*. That's displaying vulnerability!

Do understand that you will have to choose courage over comfort - you cannot have both. Perter Bergman, author of Emotional Courage, states that our feelings aren't what gets in the way; it's our reluctance to experience them. As when you are willing to feel, you are willing to act and take risks - that takes courage!

Heart

As you become to understand yourself, focusing on your self-awareness, growing on this journey - the power you will feel is in your heart. As a leader in any area of your life, you will want to use this power of the heart for inspiration and connection (social connections that stem from being self-aware).

Believe what your heart tells you, not what others say. Leading with your heart, truly feeling your intuition, allows you to show your authenticity and genuineness.

Let's write!

WORKSHEET 1

INSTRUCTIONS: Let's clear your mind. This will give you clarity on the mindset you currently posses. My friends, it can change day from day. Our goal is to stay consistent with a positive mindset and know what triggers the negative mindset and how to use it to inform us versus controlling us. Let's get started.

QUESTION #1: WHAT DOES SUCCESS LOOK LIKE?

QUESTION #2: WHAT'S STANDING IN YOUR WAY?

QUESTION #3: WHAT HAVE YOU DONE TO TRY TO SOLVE THE PROBLEM?

QUESTION #4: WHAT WILL HAPPEN IF YOU DON'T TAKE THIS STEP?

QUESTION #5: WHAT ARE YOUR NEXT STEPS MOVING FORWARD?

What are some habits you will unhook from?

"You can succeed in changing your mindset. But it takes hard work. And it is time well spent."

— Amit Ray

Daily Mindset Tracker
Use these prompts if you are not too sure what to write and to track your mindset!

ABOUT YOUR DAY

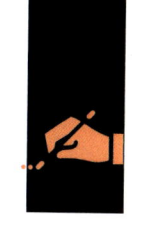

USE THESE SENTENCE STARTERS IF YOU NEED A WRITING PROMPT

COMPLETE ONE, TWO, OR ALL OF THESE LINES BELOW

DATE

Today was a good/bad day for me because...

I was excited to...

I didn't expect to...

I was disappointed because...

How was your mindset today?

JOT DOWN YOUR THOUGHTS

MINDSET IS EVERYTHING

SECTION TWO
workbook

Understanding the differences between a **fixed mindset and a growth mindset** is invaluable and puts you on the path of creating a greater impact. For us to become really good at something, it takes practice. Use this workbook as a daily reminder to practice a productive mindset...*falling in love with the journey of becoming the best version of yourself.*

If you've ever failed at reaching any goal in life, **the problem could all be in your mind.** That's how important your mindset is. **Your mind is your most powerful force.** The stories you tell yourself and the things you believe about yourself can either prevent change from happening or allow new ideas to blossom.

Your mindset can **influence your reaction and response** to the many opportunities and obstacles you encounter in your lifetime. Author Wallace D. Wattles may have put it best when he said, "Whatever you habitually think yourself to be, that you are."

Unlock your potential. Create greater impact!

Mindset is everything...why?

Others believe their basic qualities, like their intelligence or talent, are simply fixed traits. They also believe that talent alone creates success — without effort. Instead of developing their talents, they spend their lives documenting and proving themselves. **This is the growth versus fixed mindset**, discovered by Stanford University psychologist Carol Dweck. Cultivating a growth mindset can help you focus more on your most desirable goals in life. It may influence your motivation and could make you more readily able to see opportunities to learn and grow your abilities.

Unlock your potential. Create greater impact!

GROWTH MINDSET	FIXED MINDSET
✓ I can learn anything new	✘ I'm either good or I'm not
✓ My effort is the main factor that determines my abilities	✘ My abilities are predetermined by my genes
✓ With each failure, I will learn and get even better	✘ Failure shows me what I'm not good at
✓ I think that feedback is constructive and helpful	✘ Feedback is always criticism
✓ I really like to try new things	✘ I don't like to get out of my comfort zone

Mindset is everything...why?

According to the study's results, thinking and saying to oneself "I can do better next time" increases the intensity of effort people put into an activity. It can also **improve performance on any given task.**

Pay attention to your self talk and consider making changes if necessary. This is the "can-do" talk that may have a positive effect if you open yourself up to it. **It might be worth a try when you consider steps for changing your mindset. We have the power to change anything if we really want to.**

After changing your inner thought dialogue and the story you are telling yourself, you will find yourself also changing the way you talk to other people.

Write down some "can-do" talk to encourage yourself. This is an important first step in changing your mindset. Try it!

Where does Self-Talk come from? And what are Fixed Mindset Triggers?

You. It comes from you. But it is not who YOU are. Everyone has an internal voice, and part of this voice is an inner critic, inner hater, or inner doubter—**it is the fixed mindset** persona. You can hear this persona within the negative self-talk that happens in your thoughts and mind. They can trigger strong emotions and increase momentum in those emotions.

Building an awareness of your negative self-talk and recognizing every time you are giving yourself a negative message is the first step of minimizing its impact.

Every time you say something unkind to yourself, **simply write it down.**

Let's write!

"*I give myself permission to grow from my successes as well as my mistakes!*

— Nicole Smith"

<u>Daily Mindset Tracker</u>
Use these prompts if you are not too sure what to write and to track your mindset!

ABOUT YOUR DAY

USE THESE SENTENCE STARTERS IF YOU NEED A WRITING PROMPT

COMPLETE ONE, TWO, OR ALL OF THESE LINES BELOW

DATE

Today was a good/bad day for me because...

I was excited to...

I didn't expect to...

I was disappointed because...

How was your mindset today?

I give myself permission to:

JOT DOWN YOUR THOUGHTS

SECTION THREE

workbook

AFFIRMATIONS (SPEAK IT!)

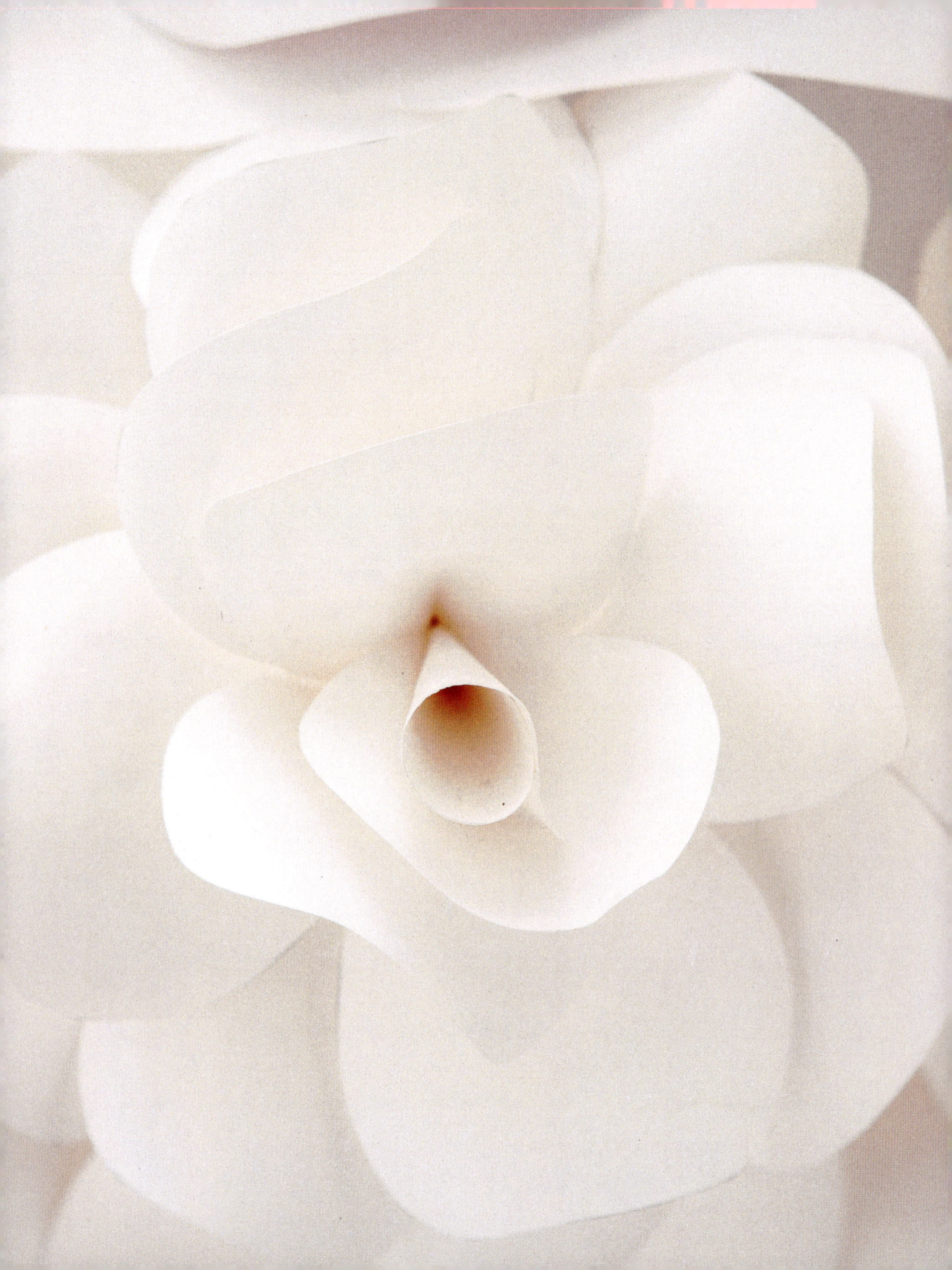

Affirmations are written or spoken positive statements that, when consistently practiced, rewire our thoughts and beliefs (and therefore emotions). Affirmations exist for all areas of your life. **A great time to repeat affirmations is just before you fall asleep and within the first couple of minutes of you waking up. Speak life and kind words to and about yourself.**

If you have a negative belief (or common thought) that causes you to feel bad, you can replace it with an empowering thought. If you repeat it to yourself regularly, such as when the negative belief is triggered AND at pre-determined times of the day, you practice this new belief, helping it become ingrained into your implicit, automatic, memory. Over time this thought becomes habituated and you **BELIEVE** it.

Plus, when focusing on the affirmative statement you direct your **FOCUS** toward what you want. This allows your brain to tune your awareness to stimulus in your environment that is a match for what you're focused on. **If you're thinking negatively, you notice negative things.**

4 Keys to Successful Affirmation Statements:

1. It must be believable and within your control.
2. It must be present tense (happening now), personal (I), positive (no "not" or "don't").
3. You must FEEL IT.
4. You must repeat it REGULARLY (3-5 times per day for 21-30 days).

Affirmations

What is a limiting belief you hold or a negative thought you say to yourself regularly that you would like to REPLACE with a more empowering, positive affirmative statement?

Incantations take affirmations a step further and make them PHYSICAL. An incantation is a phrase or language pattern that is said out loud and with an engaged physiology. Putting affirmations into motion engages more of your brain and makes it more real. It is usually repeated several times.

Speak these affirmations **OUT LOUD**. This also sends additional signals to your brain (your subconscious mind) that you are **SERIOUS**. If you are in public and don't want to draw undo attention to yourself, you say them silently—but whenever you can, say your afirmations out loud.

Next, pick a certain time that you will practice your affirmations and incantation EVERY DAY. Be specific so that it's easy to repeat and make a habit. Pick a day and time...write it here to keep yourself accountable.

> Be not afraid of growing slowly, only be afraid of standing still.
>
> – Nicole Smith

Let's write!

> "I don't chase. I attract the best income opportunities.
> — Nicole Smith"

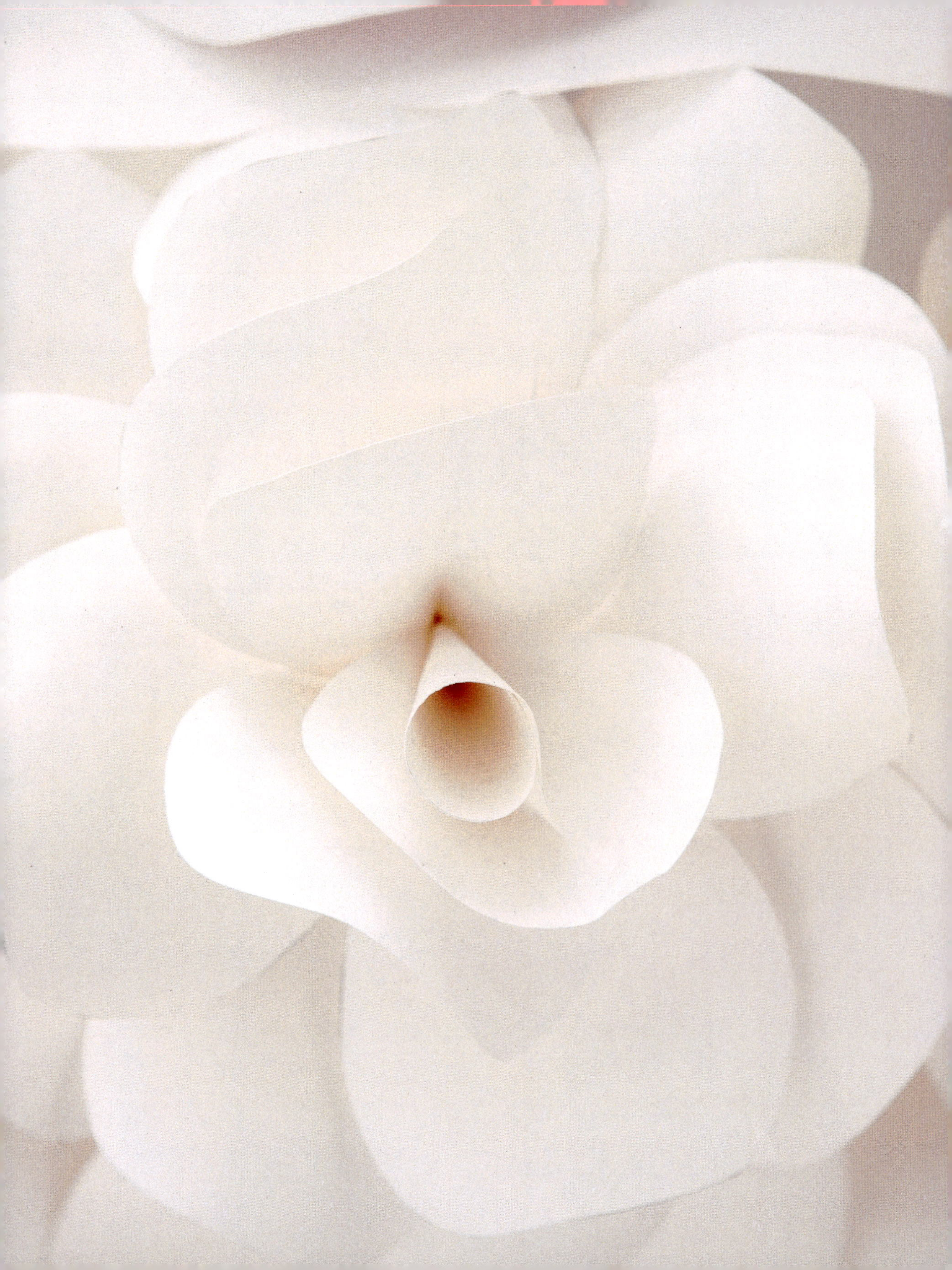

PRACTICE WORKSHEET

INSTRUCTIONS: Let's Practice: Change the negative thoughts into positive affirmations.

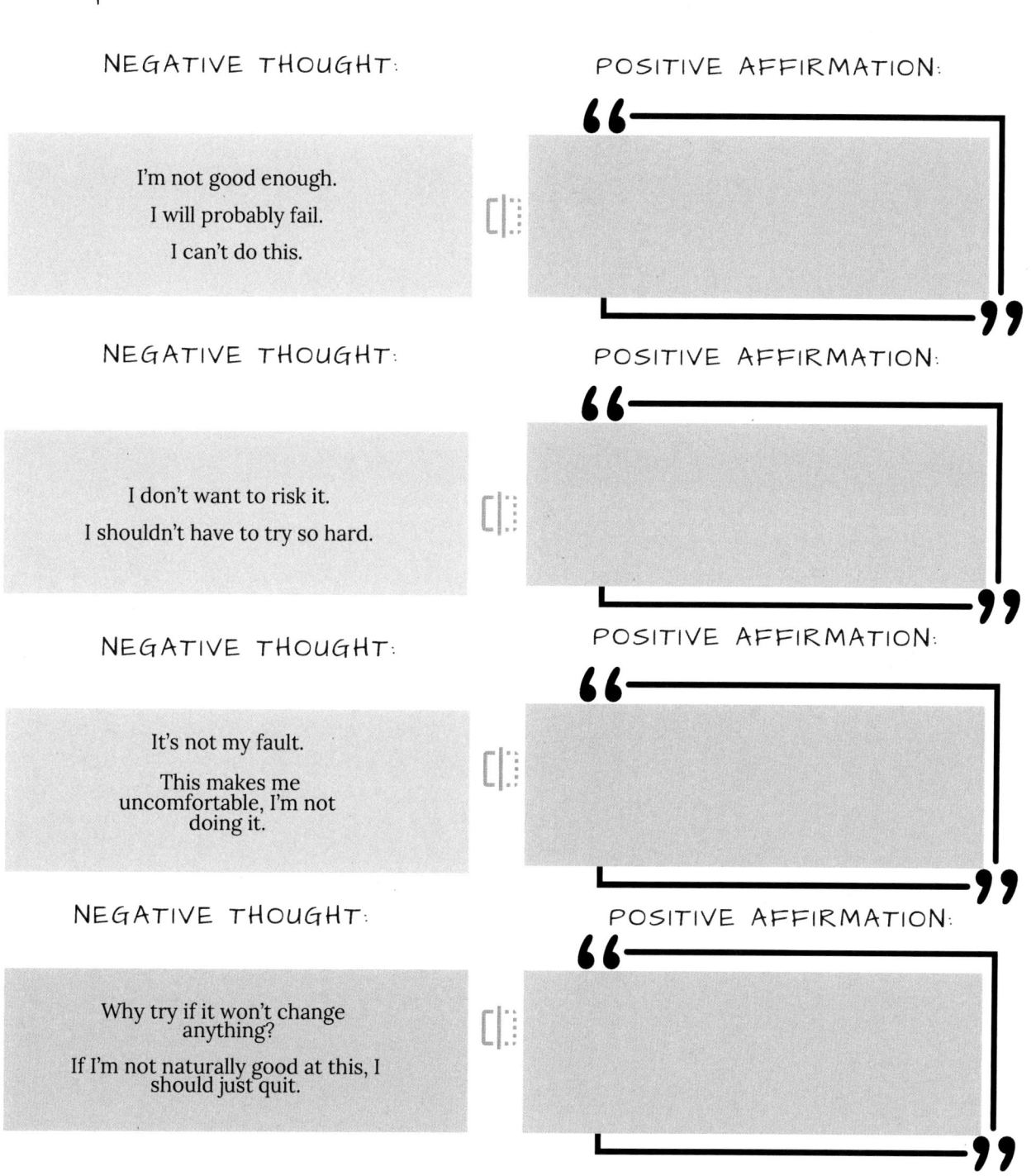

NEGATIVE THOUGHT:

I'm not good enough.
I will probably fail.
I can't do this.

POSITIVE AFFIRMATION:

" "

NEGATIVE THOUGHT:

I don't want to risk it.
I shouldn't have to try so hard.

POSITIVE AFFIRMATION:

" "

NEGATIVE THOUGHT:

It's not my fault.
This makes me uncomfortable, I'm not doing it.

POSITIVE AFFIRMATION:

" "

NEGATIVE THOUGHT:

Why try if it won't change anything?
If I'm not naturally good at this, I should just quit.

POSITIVE AFFIRMATION:

" "

WORKSHEET 3

INSTRUCTIONS: Write your negative thoughts. Change the negative thoughts into positive affirmations. Say out loud as you write them. Manifest positivity with affirming words that focus on your desires.

NEGATIVE THOUGHT: POSITIVE AFFIRMATION:

NEGATIVE THOUGHT: POSITIVE AFFIRMATION:

NEGATIVE THOUGHT: POSITIVE AFFIRMATION:

NEGATIVE THOUGHT: POSITIVE AFFIRMATION:

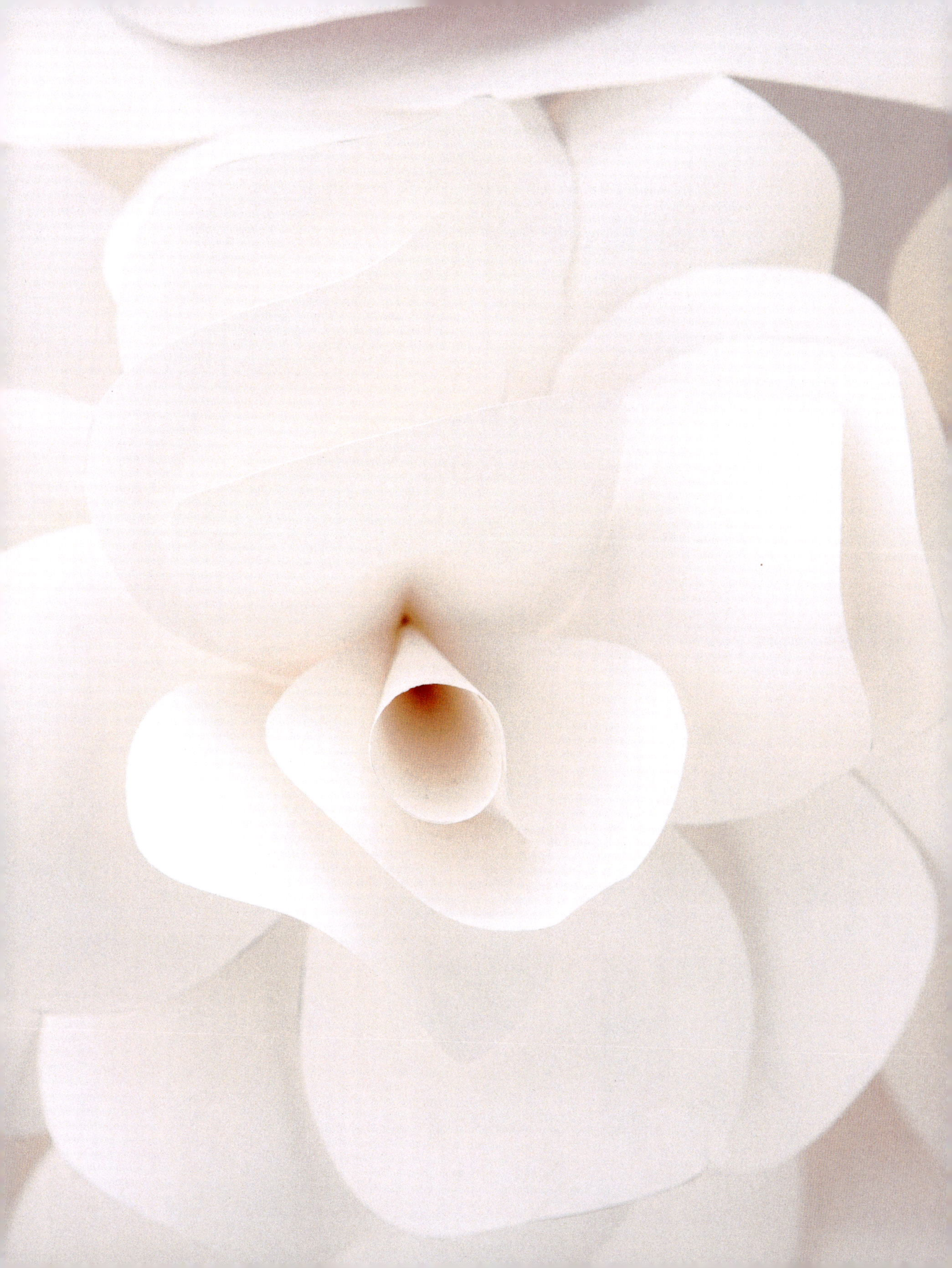

WORKSHEET 4

WRITE YOUR AFFIRMATIONS. FOR VISIBILITY, WRITE ON POST-IT NOTES AND POST IN A VISIBLE LOCATION.

See list of affirmations on the next page.

Affirmations

You can utilize any of these affirmations alone or create your own unique combination based on your personal wishes and needs. What is most important is to establish a profound communication with the universe -- so say it with conviction, say it in your own unique voice, and make it happen in the real world.

I am the architect of my life; I build its foundation and choose its contents.

Today, I am brimming with energy and overflowing with joy.

My body is healthy; my mind is brilliant; my soul is tranquil.

I am superior to negative thoughts and low actions.

I have been given endless talents which I begin to utilize today.

I forgive those who have harmed me in my past and peacefully detach from them.

A river of compassion washes away my anger and replaces it with love.

I am guided in my every step by Spirit who leads me towards what I must know and do.

(If you're married) My marriage is becoming stronger, deeper, and more stable each day.

I possess the qualities needed to be extremely successful.

Affirmations Con't

(For business owners) My business is growing, expanding, and thriving.

Creative energy surges through me and leads me to new and brilliant ideas.

Happiness is a choice. I base my happiness on my own accomplishments and the blessings I've been given.

My ability to conquer my challenges is limitless; my potential to succeed is infinite.

(For those who are unemployed) I deserve to be employed and paid well for my time, efforts, and ideas. Each day, I am closer to finding the perfect job for me.

I am courageous and I stand up for myself.

My thoughts are filled with positivity and my life is plentiful with prosperity.

Today, I abandon my old habits and take up new, more positive ones.

Many people look up to me and recognize my worth; I am admired.

I am blessed with an incredible family and wonderful friends.

I acknowledge my own self-worth; my confidence is soaring.

I acknowledge my own self-worth; my confidence is soaring.

Affirmations Con't

Everything that is happening now is happening for my ultimate good.

I am a powerhouse; I am indestructible.

Though these times are difficult, they are only a short phase of life.

My future is an ideal projection of what I envision now.

My efforts are being supported by the universe; my dreams manifest into reality before my eyes.

(For those who are single) The perfect partner for me is coming into my life sooner than I expect.

I radiate beauty, charm, and grace.

I am conquering my illness; I am defeating it steadily each day.

My obstacles are moving out of my way; my path is carved towards greatness. I wake up today with strength in my heart and clarity in my mind.

My fears of tomorrow are simply melting away.

I am at peace with all that has happened, is happening, and will happen.

My nature is Divine; I am a spiritual being.

My life is just beginning.

Daily Mindset Tracker
Use these prompts if you are not too sure what to write and to track your mindset!

ABOUT YOUR DAY

USE THESE SENTENCE STARTERS IF YOU NEED A WRITING PROMPT

COMPLETE ONE, TWO, OR ALL OF THESE LINES BELOW

DATE

Today was a good/bad day for me because...

I was excited to...

I didn't expect to...

I was disappointed because...

How was your mindset today?

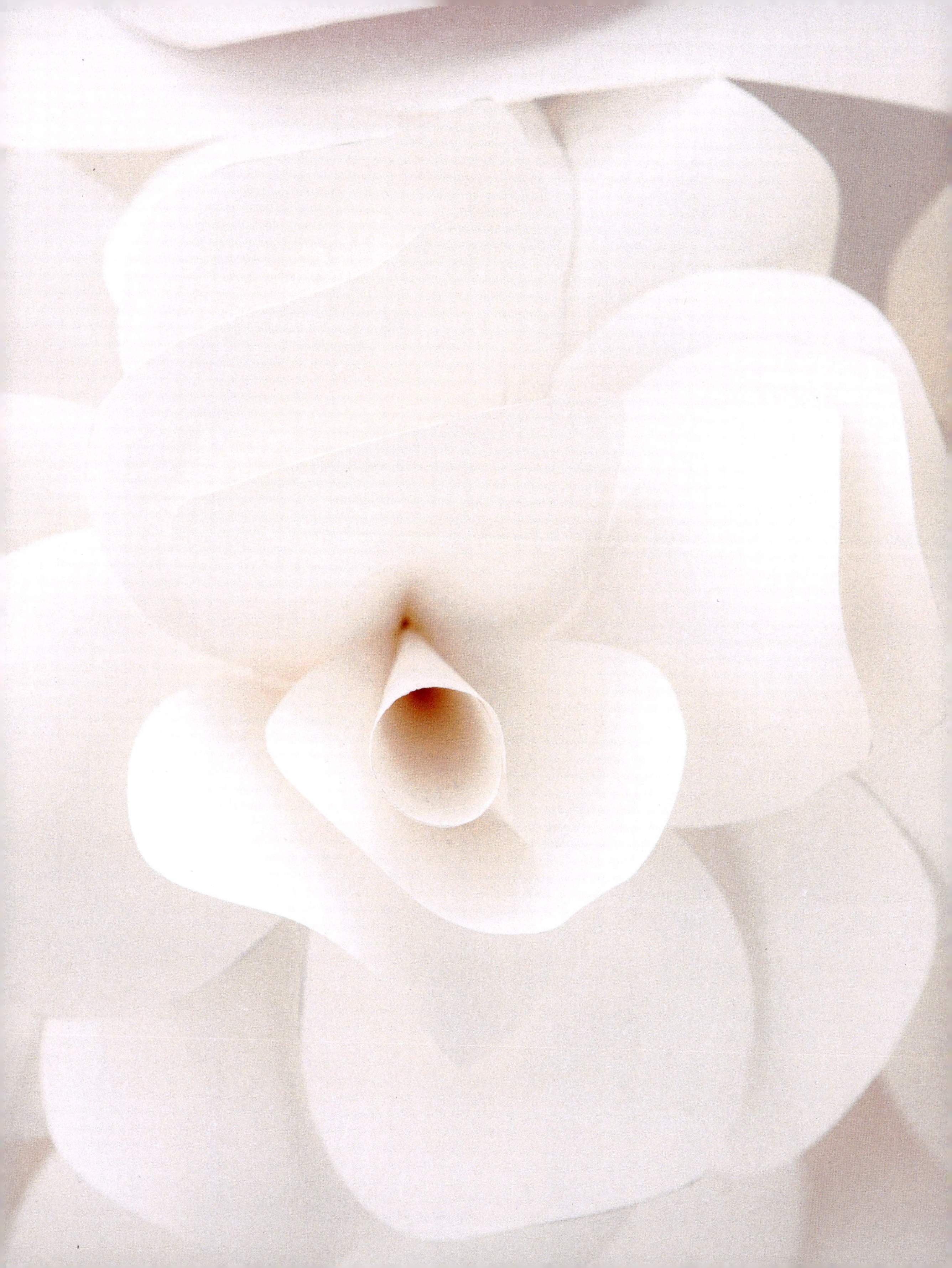

JOT DOWN YOUR THOUGHTS

Emotions affecting your mindset

SECTION FOUR
workbook

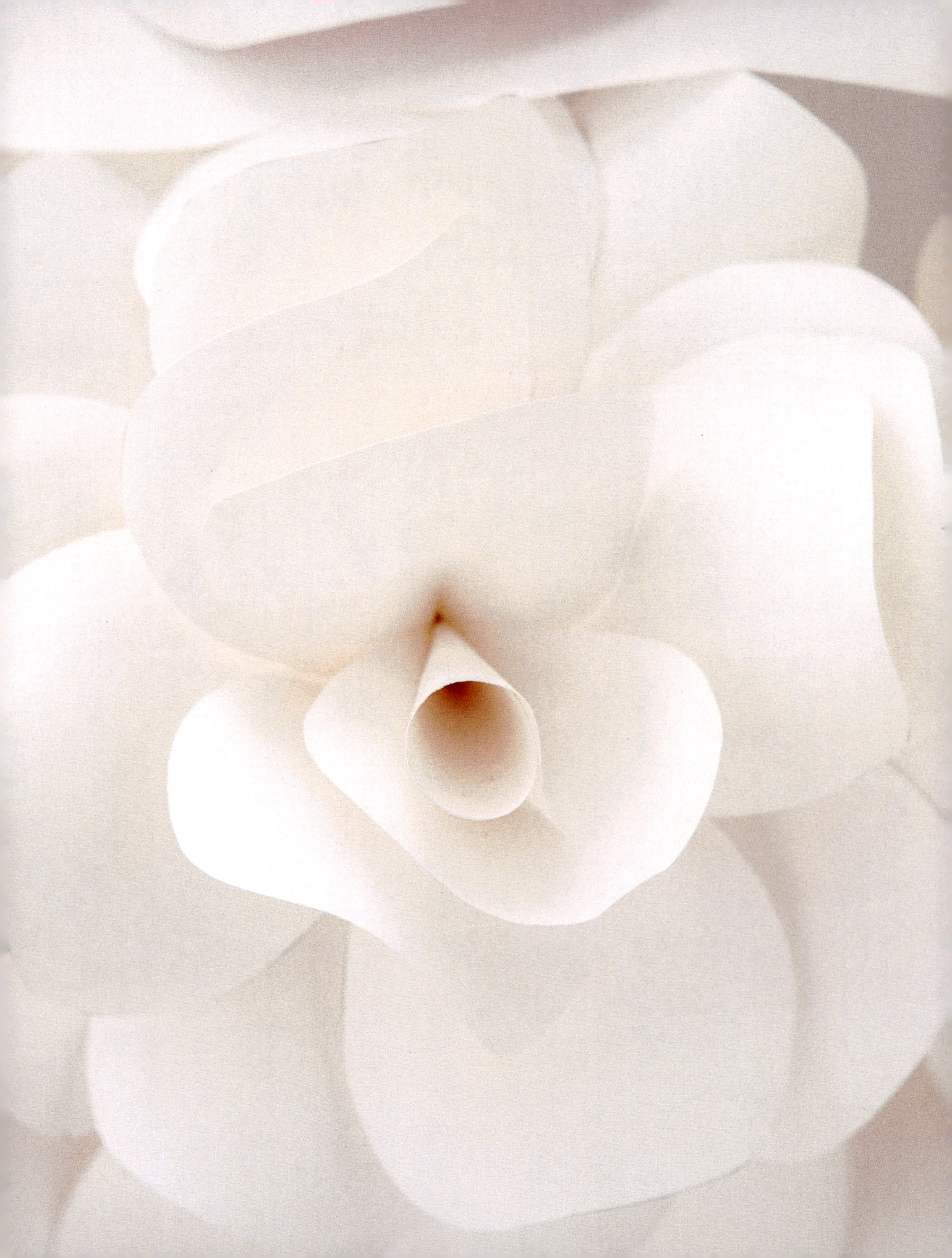

Emotional Vocabulary & Powerful Words

TRY THIS:

The next time you experience a strong emotional reaction, take time afterwards to **process not only what you're feeling, but why**. Try to put your feelings into words - the more specific the better. Now, determine what you want to do about it.

Respond appropriately vs Reacting irrationally.

EXAMPLE:

Are you angry or are you frustrated, annoyed? Are you embarrassed or are you lonely, ashamed. Are you happy or are you excited or elated?

Use specific words to describe or label your feelings, you can better "diagnose" them - helping you (and others) understand where they are coming from, and most importantly, why? The right words can help you get to the root cause of your feelings and better enable you to communicate them in a way others can understand. DO NOT judge them, however.

Tip: Focus on controlling your thoughts - self-awareness and self-management isn't only about preventing regrettable action; it also means finding a way to motivate yourself to step up and take action when doing so isn't easy, which is **Courage!**

Let's write!

"You can succeed in changing your mindset. But it takes hard work. And it is time well spent."

— Nicole Smith

WORKSHEET 5
MINDSET WORK

Write down three emotions you are feeling? Use a strong Emotional Vocabulary. Label your emotions properly. (Positive/Negative?)

Why do you feel this way? (What made you feel this way? A trigger?) Do you feel this way often? Why?

Do you feel balanced today? (Masculine Vs. Feminine Energy?)

What action do you need to take today to be your best self? What is your ONE priority today?

WORKSHEET 6

Emotional Vocabulary & Powerful Words

Write your powerful emotional word(s)! See how the words you use fall in line with your self talk which affect your mindset.

Practice your emotional vocabulary. Using the right words helps you properly label how you are feeling which will help you process the feeling.

Strive to understand each of the emotions you listed and identify how they are triggered. (positive and negative).

<u>Daily Mindset Tracker</u>
Use these prompts if you are not too sure what to write and to track your mindset!

ABOUT YOUR DAY

USE THESE SENTENCE STARTERS IF YOU NEED A WRITING PROMPT

COMPLETE ONE, TWO, OR ALL OF THESE LINES BELOW

DATE

Today was a good/bad day for me because...

I was excited to...

I didn't expect to...

I was disappointed because...

How was your mindset today?

What have you decided to focus on to help you unlock your potential?

JOT DOWN YOUR THOUGHTS

PLAN TO SHIFT YOUR MINDSET & PERSPECTIVE

SECTION FIVE
workbook

WORKSHEET 7

CHANGE YOUR PERSPECTIVE

You can make incorrect assumptions about a situation. You can interpret a situation in a negative way. Note: You may not always be able to change what happens around you, but you have a choice on how you respond react, and how you view the situation.

When you catch your fixed mindset persona (what did you name it?) with limited beliefs and negative self talk, ask yourself, what else might be going on here? Write it!

What is a more realistic and optimistic way to look at this situation? We tend to make up a story to explain what we're seeing or experiencing so we can explain to ourselves what is happening.

How can I look at this differently?

Once you become aware of an emotional reaction, negative self-talk or thoughts, you notice consequences of your point of view. You can choose to reflect on what you were thinking about the situation that caused your reaction to it.

WORKSHEET 8

CHANGE YOUR PERSPECTIVE

Ask Yourself!

What do I believe is/was going on?

What assumptions did I make about it?

Is my perspective true and how do I know it is true?

What do I not know for sure about the situation?

What other ways could I look at this?

Weekly Success Planner

My theme for this week beginning: (date)_____ is
_____

My Top 3 Priorities this week
If I did nothing else than these this week, I would be content with myself!

1.

2.

3.

My top 3 stressors/triggers
Items I need to be mindful of

1.

2

3.

Smash those Obstacles What's getting in the way? Pick one tough situation or decision you have been avoiding or procrastinating, and write one action you will take to resolve it.

Weekly Success Planner

Clearing the decks!
What will you FINISH this week?

My distractions or interruptions to watch out for this week!

What I MUST remember this week:
Any birthdays, anniversaries, things I must remember to bring, etc.

1. _____
2. _____
3. _____
4. _____

Looking After YOU! What one action will you take this week just for you?

Long-term Goal or Intention - one action I will take this week towards a long-term goal, intention or vision.

Productivity Accelerators - What actions will I take this week to accelerate my productivity.

☐ I have reviewed and balanced my organizer for the week. I have reviewed my planner. I know what I need to say "yes" and "no" to. I have allotted time and allowed plenty of time around appointments including travel time. I have time just for me, for my health and time for people important to me. My admin tasks are covered and I feel in control.

Weekly Success Planner - part 2

Your Week in Review for (date):

Progress this week? What specifically have I achieved, progressed? What are my successes and wins?

What I am proud of this week? What do I need to give myself a pat on the back for?

What have I learned this week?

Appreciation - What am I grateful for and the people I will make a point of thanking this week are:

What one thing could I do differently next week? Look at everything you've reviewed above and think of one thing you could do differently next week. It may simply be how you decide to BE or choose to see the world. It could also be an action you take, a thought or quote you focus on or something else - but it will be unique to you. Just write it here and see what happens:

Remind Yourself: How do you make an impact in this world?

Additional Writing Material

> Each next level of your life will demand a different you!
>
> — Nicole Smith

JOT DOWN YOUR THOUGHTS

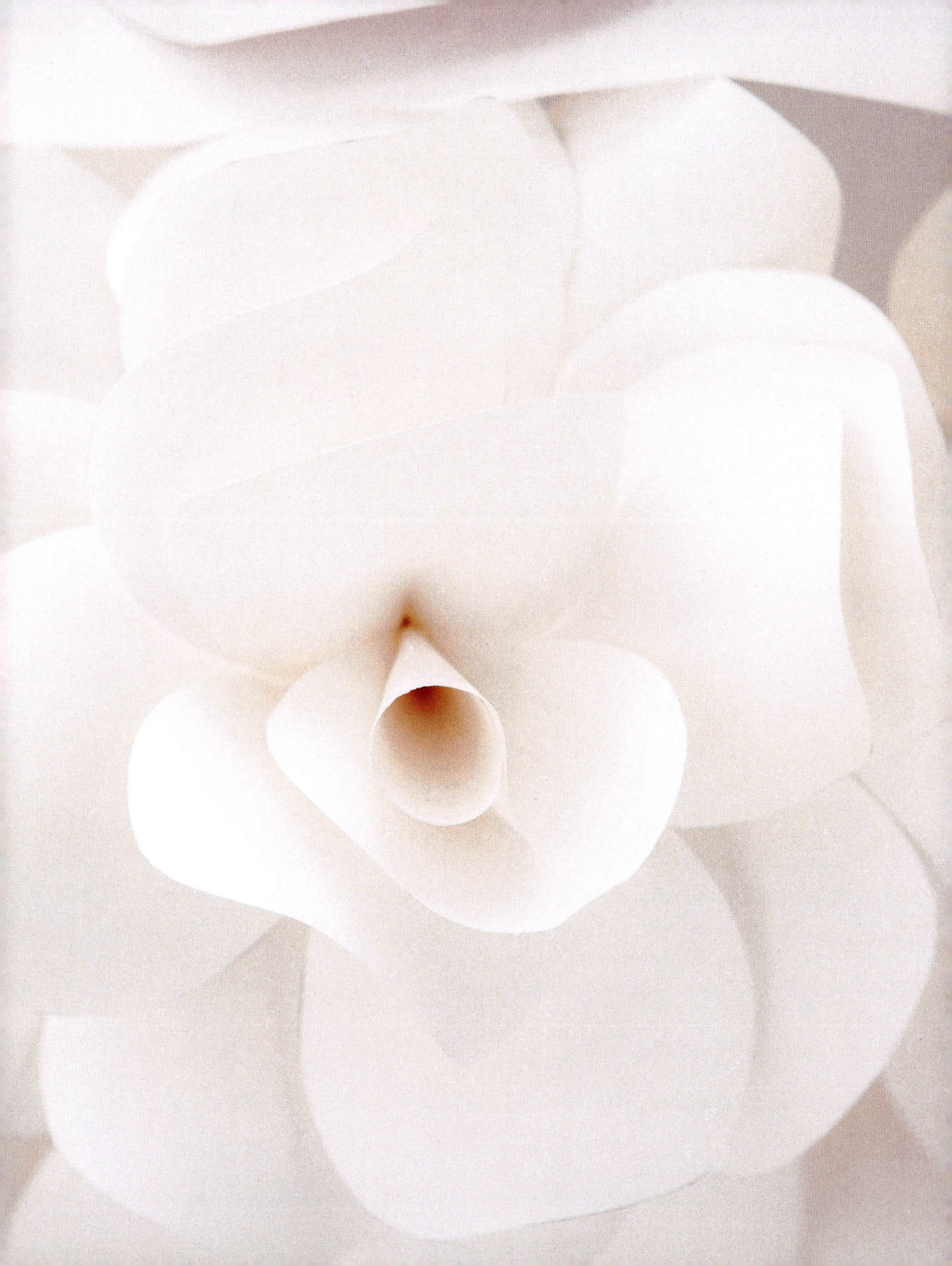

Weekly Success Planner

My theme for this week beginning: (date)_____ is
_____

My Top 3 Priorities this week
If I did nothing else than these this week, I would be content with myself!

1.

2.

3.

My top 3 stressors/triggers
Items I need to be mindful of

1.

2.

3.

Smash those Obstacles What's getting in the way? Pick one tough situation or decision you have been avoiding or procrastinating, and write one action you will take to resolve it.

Weekly Success Planner

Clearing the decks!
What will you FINISH this week?

My distractions or interruptions to watch out for this week!

What I MUST remember this week:
Any birthdays, anniversaries, things I must remember to bring, etc.

1. _____
2. _____
3. _____
4. _____

Looking After YOU! What one action will you take this week just for you?

Long-term Goal or Intention - one action I will take this week towards a long-term goal, intention or vision.

Productivity Accelerators - What actions will I take this week to accelerate my productivity.

☐ I have reviewed and balanced my organizer for the week. I have reviewed my planner. I know what I need to say "yes" and "no" to. I have allotted time and allowed plenty of time around appointments including travel time. I have time just for me, for my health and time for people important to me. My admin tasks are covered and I feel in control.

Weekly Success Planner - part 2
Your Week in Review for (date):

Progress this week? What specifically have I achieved, progressed? What are my successes and wins?

What I am proud of this week? What do I need to give myself a pat on the back for?

What have I learned this week?

Appreciation - What am I grateful for and the people I will make a point of thanking this week are:

What one thing could I do differently next week? Look at everything you've reviewed above and think of one thing you could do differently next week. It may simply be how you decide to BE or choose to see the world. It could also be an action you take, a thought or quote you focus on or something else - but it will be unique to you. Just write it here and see what happens:

Daily Mindset Tracker

Use these prompts if you are not too sure what to write and to track your mindset!

About Your Day

USE THESE SENTENCE STARTERS IF YOU NEED A WRITING PROMPT

COMPLETE ONE, TWO, OR ALL OF THESE LINES BELOW

DATE

Today was a good/bad day for me because...

I was excited to...

I didn't expect to...

I was disappointed because...

How was your mindset today?

"You asked for growth on every level, so don't be surprised when life keeps giving you opportunities to prove it."

— Nicole Smith

Weekly Success Planner

My theme for this week beginning: (date)_____ is
_____

My Top 3 Priorities this week
If I did nothing else than these this week, I would be content with myself!

1.

2.

3.

My top 3 stressors/triggers
Items I need to be mindful of

1.

2

3.

Smash those Obstacles What's getting in the way? Pick one tough situation or decision you have been avoiding or procrastinating, and write one action you will take to resolve it.

Weekly Success Planner

Clearing the decks!
What will you FINISH this week?

My distractions or interruptions to watch out for this week!

What I MUST remember this week:
Any birthdays, anniversaries, things I must remember to bring, etc.

1. _____
2. _____
3. _____
4. _____

Looking After YOU! What one action will you take this week just for you?

Long-term Goal or Intention - one action I will take this week towards a long-term goal, intention or vision.

Productivity Accelerators - What actions will I take this week to accelerate my productivity.

☐ I have reviewed and balanced my organizer for the week. I have reviewed my planner. I know what I need to say "yes" and "no" to. I have allotted time and allowed plenty of time around appointments including travel time. I have time just for me, for my health and time for people important to me. My admin tasks are covered and I feel in control.

Weekly Success Planner – part 2
Your Week in Review for (date):

Progress this week? What specifically have I achieved, progressed? What are my successes and wins?

What I am proud of this week? What do I need to give myself a pat on the back for?

What have I learned this week?

Appreciation – What am I grateful for and the people I will make a point of thanking this week are:

What one thing could I do differently next week? Look at everything you've reviewed above and think of one thing you could do differently next week. It may simply be how you decide to BE or choose to see the world. It could also be an action you take, a thought or quote you focus on or something else – but it will be unique to you. Just write it here and see what happens:

Weekly Success Planner

My theme for this week beginning: (date)_____ is
_____

My Top 3 Priorities this week
If I did nothing else than these this week, I would be content with myself!

1.

2.

3.

My top 3 stressors/triggers
Items I need to be mindful of

1.

2.

3.

Smash those Obstacles What's getting in the way? Pick one tough situation or decision you have been avoiding or procrastinating, and write one action you will take to resolve it.

Weekly Success Planner

Clearing the decks!
What will you FINISH this week?

My distractions or interruptions to watch out for this week!

What I MUST remember this week:
Any birthdays, anniversaries, things I must remember to bring, etc.

1. _____

2. _____

3. _____

4. _____

Looking After YOU! What one action will you take this week just for you?

Long-term Goal or Intention - one action I will take this week towards a long-term goal, intention or vision.

Productivity Accelerators - What actions will I take this week to accelerate my productivity.

☐ I have reviewed and balanced my organizer for the week. I have reviewed my planner. I know what I need to say "yes" and "no" to. I have allotted time and allowed plenty of time around appointments including travel time. I have time just for me, for my health and time for people important to me. My admin tasks are covered and I feel in control.

Weekly Success Planner - part 2
Your Week in Review for (date):

Progress this week? What specifically have I achieved, progressed? What are my successes and wins?

What I am proud of this week? What do I need to give myself a pat on the back for?

What have I learned this week?

Appreciation - What am I grateful for and the people I will make a point of thanking this week are:

What one thing could I do differently next week? Look at everything you've reviewed above and think of one thing you could do differently next week. It may simply be how you decide to BE or choose to see the world. It could also be an action you take, a thought or quote you focus on or something else - but it will be unique to you. Just write it here and see what happens:

Weekly Success Planner

My theme for this week beginning: (date)_____ is
_____

My Top 3 Priorities this week
If I did nothing else than these this week, I would be content with myself!

1.

2.

3.

My top 3 stressors/triggers
Items I need to be mindful of

1.

2

3.

Smash those Obstacles What's getting in the way? Pick one tough situation or decision you have been avoiding or procrastinating, and write one action you will take to resolve it.

Weekly Success Planner

Clearing the decks!
What will you FINISH this week?

My distractions or interruptions to watch out for this week!

What I MUST remember this week:
Any birthdays, anniversaries, things I must remember to bring, etc.

1. _____
2. _____
3. _____
4. _____

Looking After YOU! What one action will you take this week just for you?

Long-term Goal or Intention - one action I will take this week towards a long-term goal, intention or vision.

Productivity Accelerators - What actions will I take this week to accelerate my productivity.

☐ I have reviewed and balanced my organizer for the week. I have reviewed my planner. I know what I need to say "yes" and "no" to. I have allotted time and allowed plenty of time around appointments including travel time. I have time just for me, for my health and time for people important to me. My admin tasks are covered and I feel in control.

Weekly Success Planner - part 2
Your Week in Review for (date):

Progress this week? What specifically have I achieved, progressed? What are my successes and wins?

What I am proud of this week? What do I need to give myself a pat on the back for?

What have I learned this week?

Appreciation - What am I grateful for and the people I will make a point of thanking this week are:

What one thing could I do differently next week? Look at everything you've reviewed above and think of one thing you could do differently next week. It may simply be how you decide to BE or choose to see the world. It could also be an action you take, a thought or quote you focus on or something else - but it will be unique to you. Just write it here and see what happens:

Daily Mindset Tracker
Use these prompts if you are not too sure what to write and to track your mindset!

ABOUT YOUR DAY

USE THESE SENTENCE STARTERS IF YOU NEED A WRITING PROMPT

COMPLETE ONE, TWO, OR ALL OF THESE LINES BELOW

DATE

Today was a good/bad day for me because...

I was excited to...

I didn't expect to...

I was disappointed because...

How was your mindset today?

<u>Daily Mindset Tracker</u>
Use these prompts if you are not too sure what to write and to track your mindset!

ABOUT YOUR DAY

USE THESE SENTENCE STARTERS IF YOU NEED A WRITING PROMPT

COMPLETE ONE, TWO, OR ALL OF THESE LINES BELOW

DATE

Today was a good/bad day for me because...

I was excited to...

I didn't expect to...

I was disappointed because...

How was your mindset today?

<u>Daily Mindset Tracker</u>
Use these prompts if you are not too sure what to write and to track your mindset!

ABOUT YOUR DAY

USE THESE SENTENCE STARTERS IF YOU NEED A WRITING PROMPT

COMPLETE ONE, TWO, OR ALL OF THESE LINES BELOW

DATE

Today was a good/bad day for me because...

I was excited to...

I didn't expect to...

I was disappointed because...

How was your mindset today?

<u>Daily Mindset Tracker</u>
Use these prompts if you are not too sure what to write and to track your mindset!

ABOUT YOUR DAY

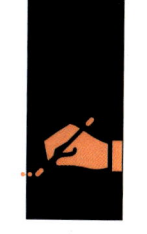

USE THESE SENTENCE STARTERS IF YOU NEED A WRITING PROMPT

COMPLETE ONE, TWO, OR ALL OF THESE LINES BELOW

DATE

Today was a good/bad day for me because...

I was excited to...

I didn't expect to...

I was disappointed because...

How was your mindset today?

JOT DOWN YOUR THOUGHTS